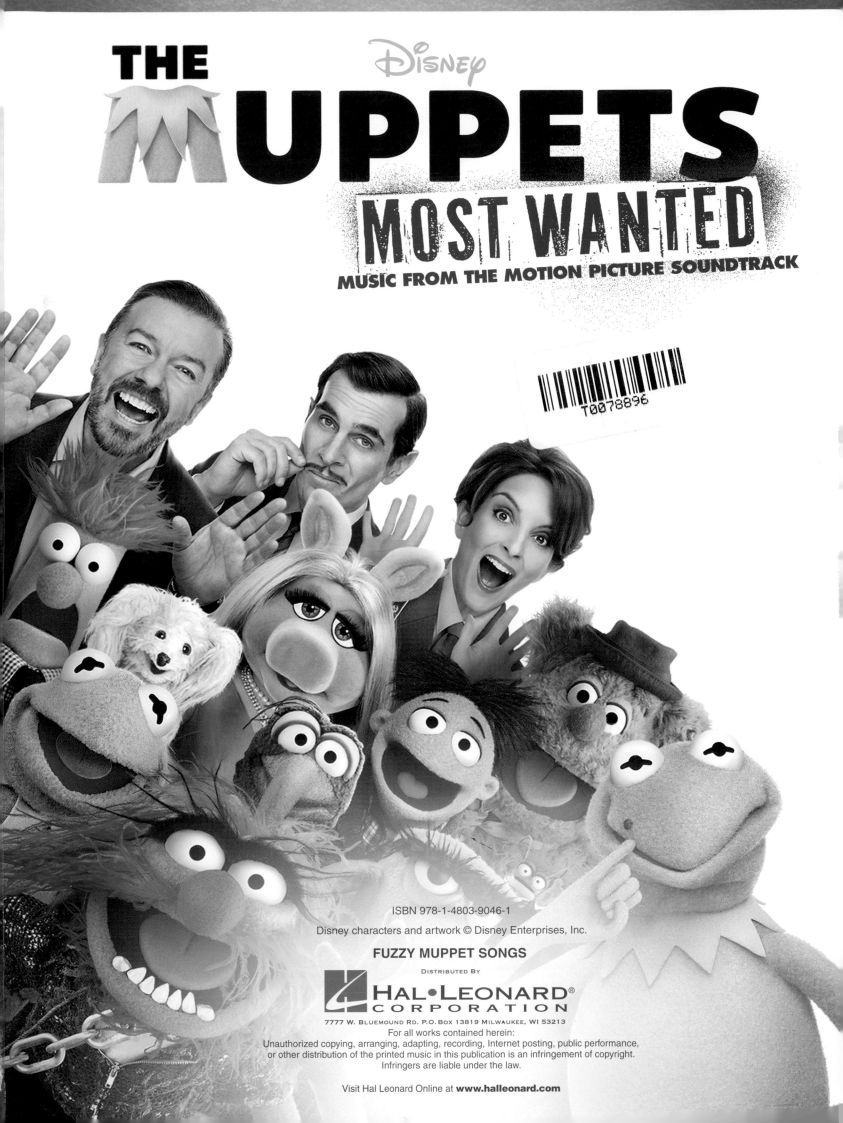

PIANO · VOCAL · GUITAR

Disney

THE MUPPETS

MOST WANTED

MUSIC FROM THE MOTION PICTURE SOUNDTRACK

T0078896

ISBN 978-1-4803-9046-1

Disney characters and artwork © Disney Enterprises, Inc.

FUZZY MUPPET SONGS

DISTRIBUTED BY

HAL•LEONARD®
CORPORATION

7777 W. BLUEMOUND RD. P.O. BOX 13819 MILWAUKEE, WI 53213

Visit Hal Leonard Online at **www.halleonard.com**

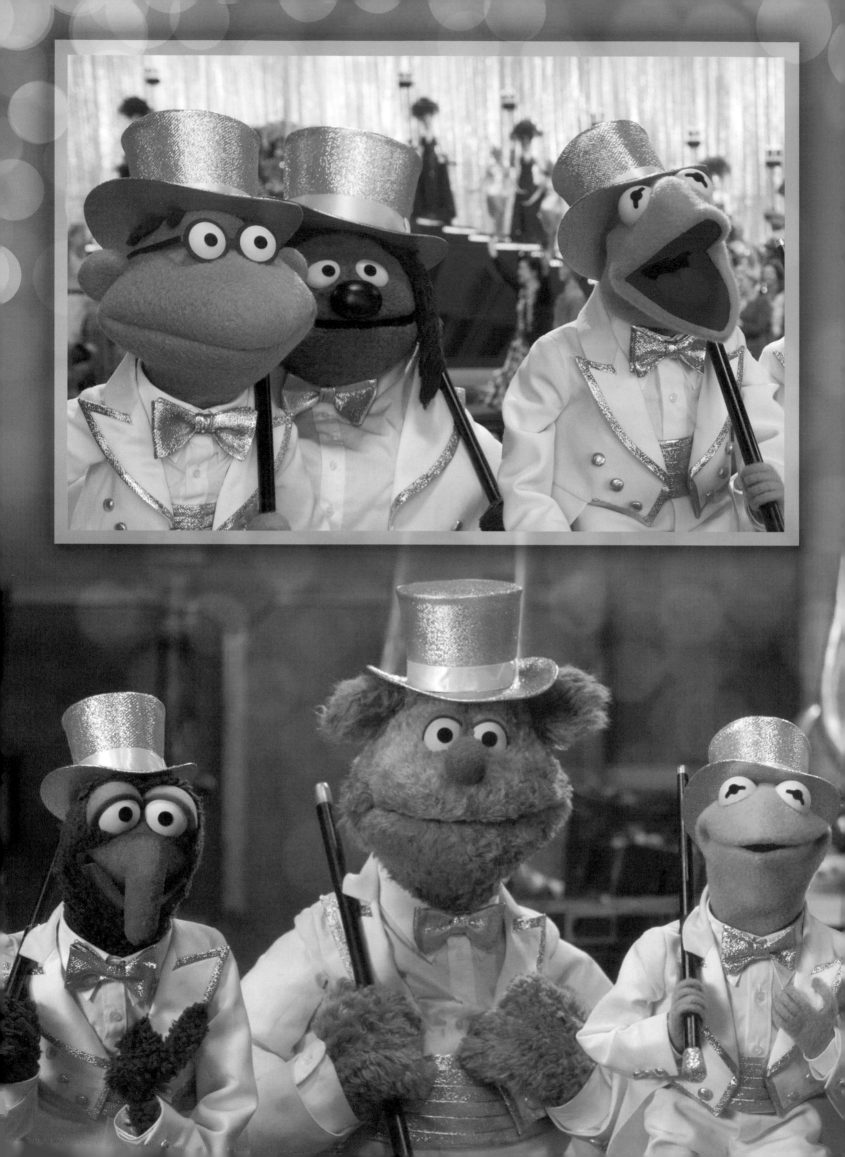

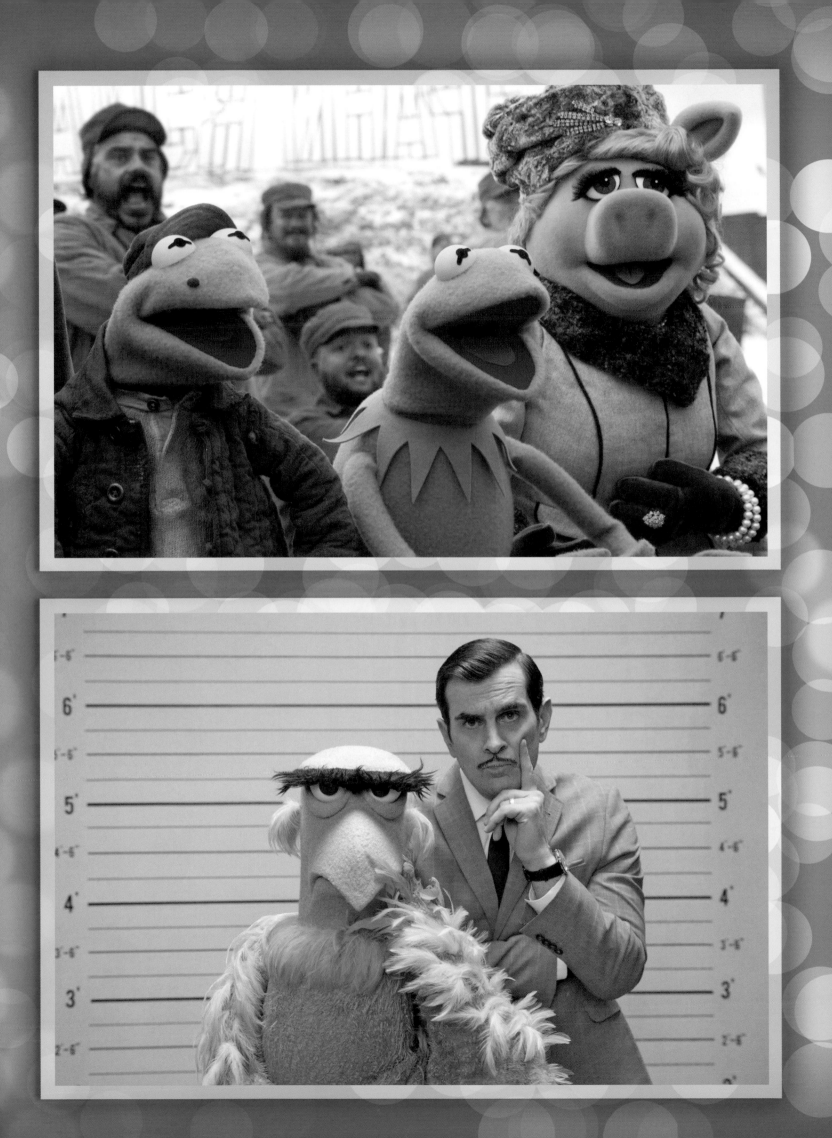

WE'RE DOING A SEQUEL

Music and Lyrics by
BRET McKENZIE

PIGGY: The stu-di-o con-sid-ers us a

vi-a-ble fran-chise. KERMIT, FOZZIE, SCOOTER, PIGGY & ROWLF: We're do-ing a se-quel.

ROWLF: How hard can it be? We

can't do an-y worse than the God-fa-ther Three.

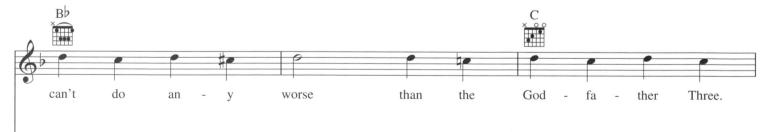

I'M NUMBER ONE

Music and Lyrics by
BRET McKENZIE

mat-ter of time _ be-fore he's gone and I'm at the front of the line.

It won't be long 'til I'll get my chance, _ but in the mean-time I've got to

dance, mon-key, dance.

CONSTANTINE:

Dance, mon-key, dance! _

Now watch me...

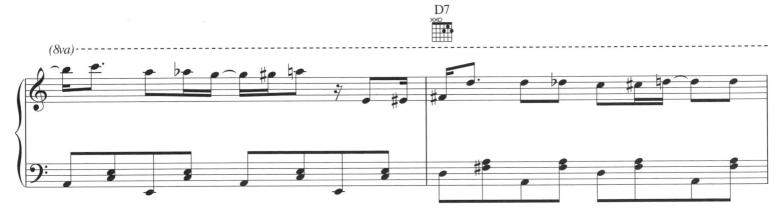

DOMINIC: (He's num - ber one.) __
I'm num - ber one, you're num - ber

(I'm num - ber two.) __ Ha! That's it, kid, there you go. Now
two. __

THE BIG HOUSE

Music and Lyrics by
BRET McKENZIE

Big House you will not sur - vive. ___ When you ar - rive ___ in the

Big House, run ___ for your life! ___ NADYA:

(Mouth trumpet solo ad lib.)

I'LL GET YOU WHAT YOU WANT
(Cockatoo in Malibu)

Music and Lyrics by
BRET McKENZIE

Moderately fast

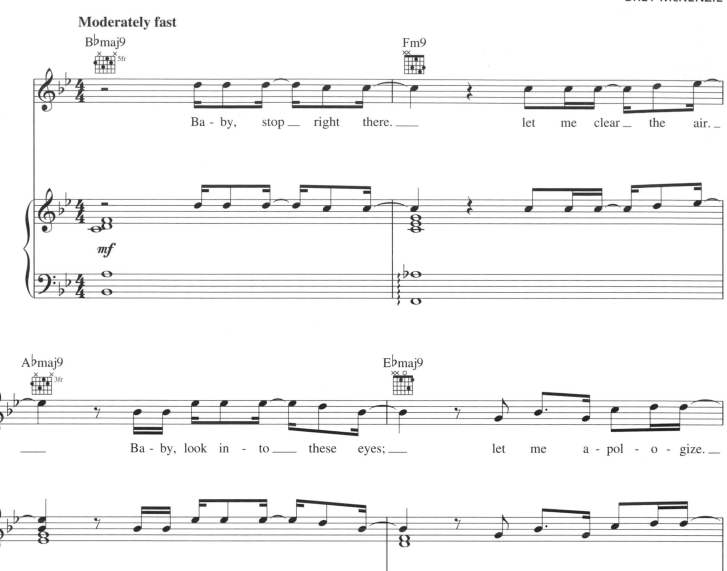

Ba - by, stop right there. ___ let me clear the air. ___

Ba - by, look in - to ___ these eyes; ___ let me a - pol - o - gize. ___

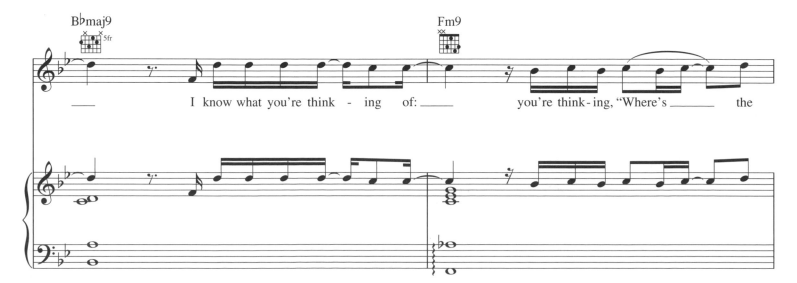

I know what you're think - ing of: ___ you're think - ing, "Where's ___ the

THE MUPPET SHOW THEME

Words and Music by JIM HENSON
and SAM POTTLE

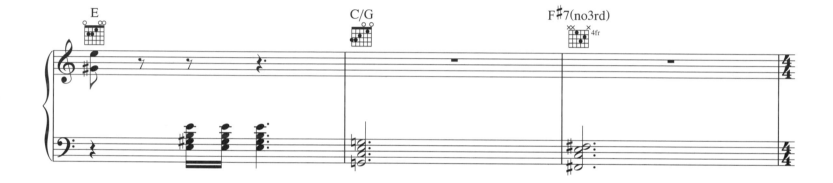

FEMALE MUPPETS:

Que em - pie - ce

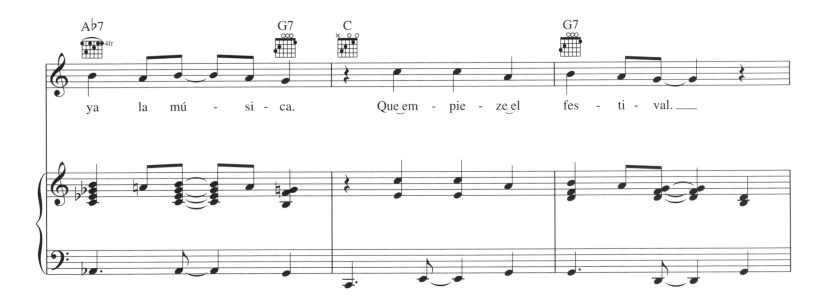

ya la mú - si - ca. Que em - pie - ze el fes - ti - val. ___

Ya es - tán a - quí Los Mup - pets es - te

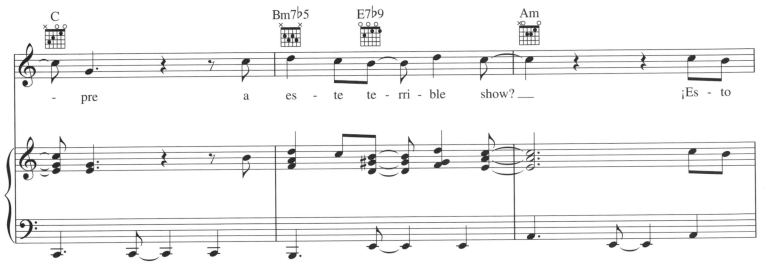

-pre a es - te te - rri - ble show? __ ¡Es - to

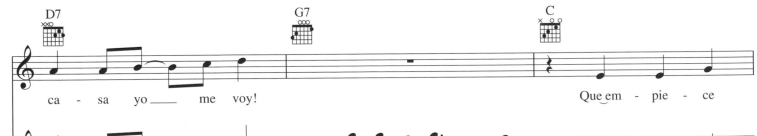

es u - na tor - tu - ra _____ y a

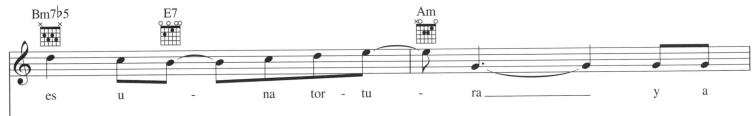

ca - sa yo __ me voy! Que em - pie - ce

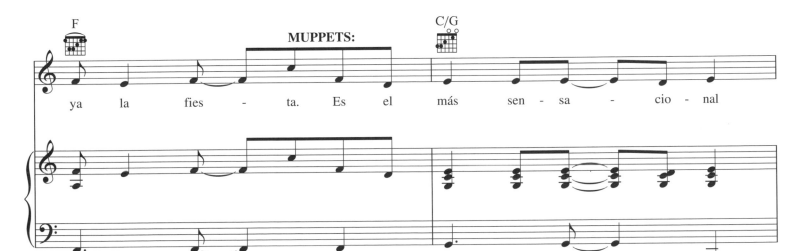

MUPPETS:

ya la fies - ta. Es el más sen - sa - cio - nal

INTERROGATION SONG

Music by BRET McKENZIE
Lyrics by BRET McKENZIE and PAUL ROEMEN

SOMETHING SO RIGHT

Music and Lyrics by
BRET McKNEZIE

why do I feel I don't _____ know you?

MISS PIGGY & KERMIT:

We'll set - tle down and start a fam - i - ly, have a min - i you and a

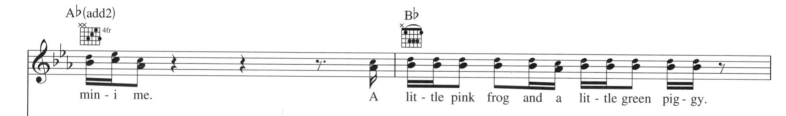

min - i me. A lit - tle pink frog and a lit - tle green pig - gy.

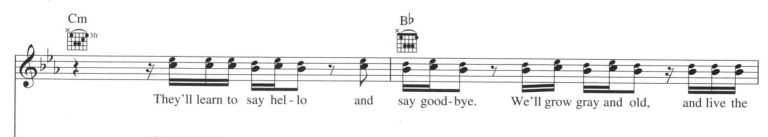

They'll learn to say hel - lo and say good-bye. We'll grow gray and old, and live the

MISS PIGGY:

Af - ter all ___ we've been through, ___

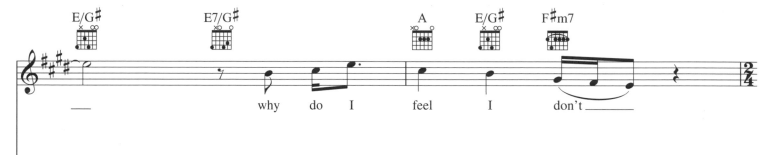

— why do I feel I don't ___

know you?

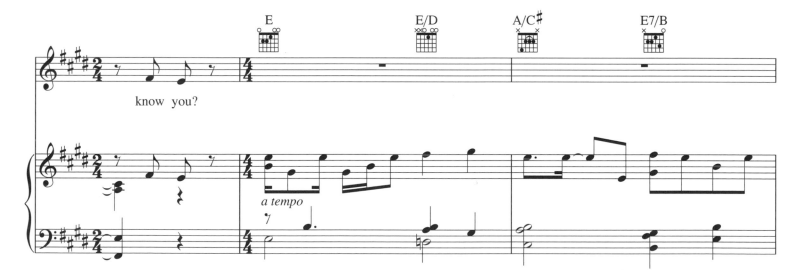

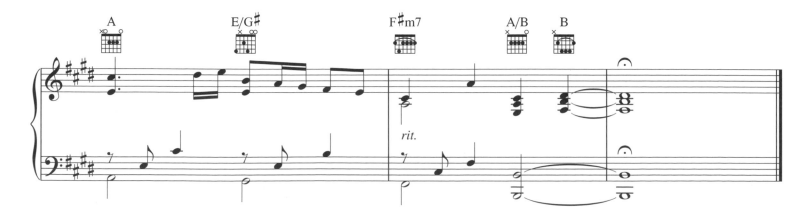

WORKING IN THE COAL MINE

Words and Music by
ALLEN TOUSSAINT

Five o'-clock in the morn - in', I'm al - read - y up and gone.
'Cause I make ear - ly morn - in', haul - in' coal by the

ton. But when Sat - ur - day rolls a - round, I'm

Lord, I'm so ti - red,

1

How long can this go on? I've been too tired for hav - in' fun.

2

D.S. al Coda

I'm just

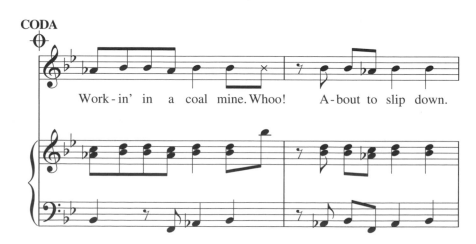

CODA

Work - in' in a coal mine. Whoo! A - bout to slip down.

(Spoken:) Lord! I'm so tired! How long can this

go on? I'm just work-in' in a coal mine,
Work-in' in a coal mine,

Repeat and Fade

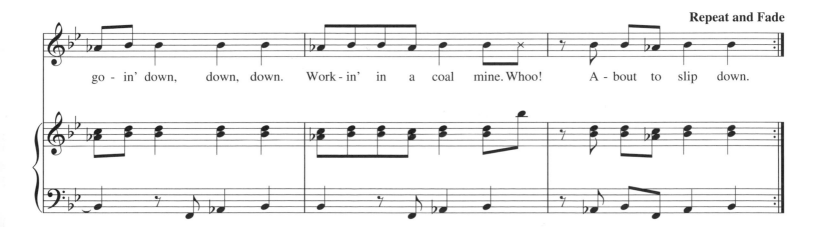

go - in' down, down, down. Work-in' in a coal mine. Whoo! A - bout to slip down.

TOGETHER AGAIN

Words and Music by
JEFF MOSS

ISOLATION BOX/ JOSH GROBAN:

Heh! Heh! I just can't i - mag - ine that you've ev - er been gone! __ It's not start - ing o - ver, it's just go - ing on. __

ALL:

To - geth - er a - gain, a - gain. Gee, it's good to be to - geth - er a - gain, a - gain. 'Cause

MOVES LIKE JAGGER

Words and Music by ADAM LEVINE,
BENJAMIN LEVIN, AMMAR MALIK
and JOHAN SCHUSTER

With energy and a groove

Oh, ___ now.

Oh.   Just shoot for the stars _

if it feels _____ right, and aim for my heart _____
when you feel _____ like you're bro-ken and scarred, _____

if you feel _____ like it. Take me a - way _____
noth - in' feels _____ right. But when you're with me, _____

and make it o - kay, _____ I swear I'll be - have. _____
I'll make you be - lieve _____ that I've got the key. _____

You want - ed con - trol, _____ so we wait -
Oh, so get in the car, _____ we can ride _____

-ed. I put on a show, ___ now we're na - ked. You say I'm a kid, ___
___ it wher - ev - er you want, ___ get in - side ___ it. And you wan - na steer, ___

Cm7

___ my e - go is big. ___ I don't give a sh**. ___
___ but I'm shift - in' gear. ___ I'll take it from here. ___

Gm7

And it goes ___ like this: ___ Take me by the tongue and I'll know ___ you.

Cm7

Kiss me on the cheek and I'll show ___ you all the moves like Jag - ger. I've got the

moves like Jag - ger. I've got the moves _____ like Jag - ger.

I don't need to try to con - trol __ you. Look in - to my eyes

and I'll own __ you with them moves like Jag - ger. I've got the moves like Jag - ger. I've got the

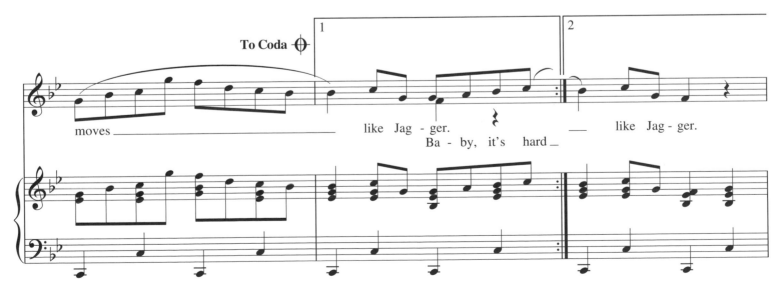

moves _____ like Jag - ger.

like Jag - ger.
Ba - by, it's hard __

Head to toe, oh, ba-by, rub me right.___ But___ if I share my se - cret,___

___ you're gon - na have to keep it._____ No - bod - y else can see this,___

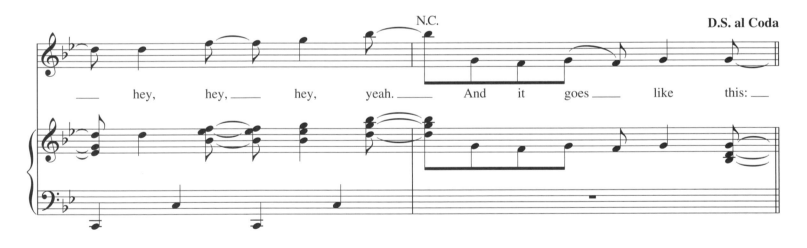

___ hey, hey,___ hey, yeah.___ And it goes___ like this:___

___ like Jag - ger.

MACARENA

Words and Music by ANTONIO ROMERO
and RAFAEL RUIZ

Moderately

(Ay! Ay!)

(Ay! Ay!)

(Ay! Ay!)

MISS PIGGY:
(Ay! Ay!) When I dance _ they call _ me Ma-ca-re-na,

and the boys,_ they say,_ "Que soy bue-na!" They all want me, they can't have me,

so they all come and dance be-side me. Move with me, chat with me,

and if you're good I'll take_ you home with me. Move with me, chat with me,

FELLAS:

and if you're good I'll let_ you dance with me. Da-le a tu cuer-po a-le-gri-a, Ma-ca-re-na. Que tu

Da - le a tu cuer-po a - le - gri - a, Ma - ca - re - na. Hey, ___ Ma - ca - re - na. (Ay! Ay!)

E5 Bm7 B5 E5 Bm7 B5

Da - le a tu cuer-po a - le - gri - a, Ma - ca - re - na. Que tu cuer-po es pa' dar - le a - le - gri - a y co - sa bue - na.

E5 Bm7 B5 E5 Bm7 B5

Da - le a tu cuer-po a - le - gri - a, Ma - ca - re - na. Hey, ___ Ma - ca - re - na. (Ay! Ay!)

E5

MISS PIGGY:

(laughs)

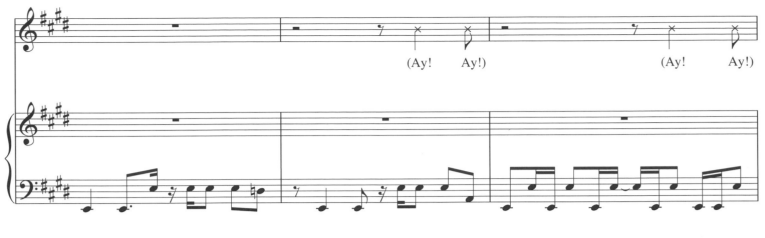

(Ay! Ay!) (Ay! Ay!)

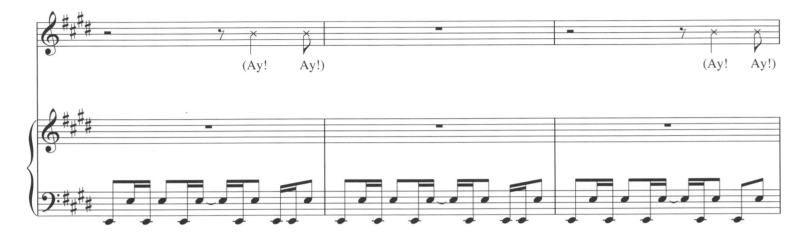

(Ay! Ay!) (Ay! Ay!)

E5

Come and find _ me. My name is Ma-ca-re-na. Al-ways at the par-ty con las chi-cas es-tan bue-nas.

Come join me! Dance with me! And all you fel-las chant_ a-long with me.